I0142545

WILD HORSES

KATHLEEN PATRICK

KATYDIDIT PUBLISHING

For the people within these pages who are no longer with us and for their families. Because in the end, all we have are stories and love.

"She had some horses she loved.
She had some horses she hated.
These were the same horses."

She Had Some Horses by Joy Harjo

CONTENTS

ABOUT THIS BOOK

"Kathleen Patrick portrays humanity at its flawed worst and inspiring best."

From the best-selling author of *Airmail: A Story of War in Poems* and *So Many Wings*, comes *Wild Horses*, a riveting collection of poetry that reminds the reader that being human is tricky business. And in the end, all we have are stories and love.

Wild Horses explores Patrick's love/hate relationship with horses from childhood through adulthood as a metaphor for some of life's most difficult challenges. Her work spans the spectrum of emotions from elation, celebration, and joy, to anxiety, grief, and despair.

As in her past books, each poem tells a story, and each story flows effortlessly into the next. Through simple language and beautiful detail, she takes us along for the ride.

"Patrick's voice will stay with you long after you read the last page."

PART I

JUN · 63 J ·

INDELIBLE DRUMS

I.

Our house was a trailer

with two bedrooms, bunk beds

for my brother and me.

At night I prayed out loud with my mother

that my guardian angel would watch over me,

but secretly, I knew all along

it was really an owl,

a massive bird somewhere

in the dark beyond my covers.

When I pushed my fingers

into the corners of my closed eyes,

I could see his,

fleeting yellow hoops,

suspended in the night.

Tumbleweeds collected near the trailer,
made it seem rooted down. At age five,
I walked the two blocks to main street,
took a postcard of a Palomino
from the drugstore because
I thought they were free.
Mother smiled,
sent me back with a nickel.
I saved that splendid horse,
decided to ride him
into the rest of my life.

Sunday mornings, playing in our dirt yard,
I watched the men bent low
over short-handled brooms,
heard the scratch of sand.
Sioux men swept the streets
of that reservation town, after the sheriff
sold them liquor on Saturday,
then arrested them when they were drunk.
This, I learned later.
All I remember of the sheriff
is his too big belly

and round white pillars
on the porch of his house.

II.

Because I wanted to go back,
to sort memory from real dust,
we drove the washboard roads
into a grassland basin
painted brown by grasshoppers
and fierce sun.
My friend and I,
wasi'chu at a powwow;
white women in the middle
of something else.
Tarps shaded elders
as they spoke in Lakota.
Dancers wore powerful feathers
of proud birds,
wore buckskin and beads
because they told stories,
stepped forward and back in time,
in the yellowed grass
of the circle.

The circle.

The place where the drums and

the singers swept the sky

with ancient voices,

feeling the sacred music

with a rhythm

that came from the Hills,

from the Black Hills

where the drums began.

DIRECTIONS

The beadworker?

She may be in Wakpala,

if she's still alive.

Has a box of beads

the colors of time.

Small squares in a

wooden box

divide the colors

her sleeping eyes

don't see.

Grandchildren help with them beads,

sort the colors then watch her

find the truth in patterns.

She's the best.

Do you understand?

Look her up.

Maybe she'll invite you in,

give you a hot cup of tea.

POSTCARD TO MOTHER IN ALASKA

You fled to the Kenai Peninsula
surrounded by mountains older than grief,
to catch salmon, you said. To feel
the reel in your hands like an answer,
and who knows. It has not rained
since you left. Everything turns brown
as I grow round and tired.
Do you want to come home?
I am teaching your grandson to swim.
We cling to each other in the cool envelope
of buoyancy. He is ready for the new baby.
I am surrounded by water. I am
ready for anything. Send word.

PERMISSION

If it is all right—
if I may talk to you—
if I may say anything—
if I may talk and say
whatever I please—I will—
please say it's all right—I
need permission—I am
still your child—I am still
your child—I still need permission—
if it's all right to need you—
to say it's all right—to say I need you—to
say anything I want to—say that to me—
say whatever you want—say you want me to need you—
say you don't—say whatever you want—

say you need me—say I am still your child—

I am still your child—say it—

you have my permission.

FRAGILE HEARTS

If I offer you tulips in spring,

the ones I planted,

the ones you showed me how to plant

in front of my happy house,

will they cheer you?

Those fragile red and yellow hearts,

attached only at the center.

A robust wind could send them

over the edge.

You've grown tired of living.

Now only my children

sit full center,

holding on to you,

keeping you together.

What can I offer you?

My happiness sits like a granite pill

in my mouth. I swallow the stone whole.

I am lucky and yet.

The color of my tulips

burns deep in the cradle of your neck

as you turn away from him to sleep—

to spend the spring sleeping.

What can I give you?

My children, yes, such joy

your knots come loose

as you love them in circles.

Bedtime stories again and again

until you all can sleep.

LONG WALK ON STANDING ROCK

I.

My father coached basketball in nineteen sixty-one
on the flat brownness of South Dakota.
He taught high school science
and took me to school on Sundays to correct papers.
The tables were tall and had black shiny tops
like the backs of crickets.
He showed me where they were growing mold
on bread, discovering the course of medicine.
There was an ant farm too.
The glass sides were so close together
I wondered how they ever turned around
if they happened to change their minds.

∼

It was all right with the townspeople

to have Indian kids on the team

as long as they were scoring points

and winning games and not taking anything

whatsoever away from the white kids.

The crowd would boo when Willard Male Bear

went into the game. Then, like slowly deflating balloons,

they would watch his athletic magic

and pretend not to notice

that he arced the winning shot.

∾

Before games, athletes were welcomed

at our trailer house for a bowl of soup.

After practice, it might be a warm coat,

for the long walk into cold darkness.

When Mother recalls those years,

the boy she remembers is Willard.

Not quiet, but nearly speechless. He said

three or four words the whole year.

Stood at the door of the trailer the night

of a high school dance with a white shirt.

"Iron," he said gently, holding it out to her.

∾

The story I remember most

is of the knotting kind. The kind

that eats away at faith.

My father was hospitalized for pneumonia.

Willard walked the nineteen miles to town

to buy a card, took it to the hospital

and wasn't allowed in

because he was an Indian.

He could not walk down the hall

with the small white envelope

addressed to "Coach" in careful script writing,

could not hand it to him,

across the cotton sheets

and say hello or not say hello,

could not make the choice,

had no choice,

walked the nineteen miles home.

Did he look at anyone as he passed through town?

Did anyone look at him?

Did he feel the warmth of the sun on his back?

Did he hear the sounds of the town

as he put it behind him?

Could he hear birds?

Were there birds in the trees?

Was he listening to the gravel

grinding beneath his feet?

How did the road feel on his feet?

Did he pass any farms?

Did he notice the white clapboard houses?

Were there cows and horses

standing in the shade of red barns?

Did he think about the fences?

Did he notice the wealth was white?

Did his feet hurt when he got home?

Were his brothers and sisters awake?

Was his mother still at the loom?

Was she weaving?

Did he talk to her?

Did he tell her anything

about what had happened to his life?

II.

Telephone Call to My Father

Tell me the story again.

Do I have it right?

Was it 1968? Did it happen

in the middle of reservation land?

An old student of yours

at a cheap honkytonk and

too much beer.

And the guy who stabbed him—

was he white? Was he drunk?

Did he live in town?

What did Willard say, exactly?

How did it happen?

I remember hearing he was sliced clear across

the stomach and the hospital in town

turned him down—on reservation land—right?

Stabbed in the stomach,

he had to be driven twenty-seven miles

to Fort Yates to the Indian hospital,

is that correct?

I want to know who turned him away.

Was it a nurse at the desk?

Was it a janitor in the emergency waiting room?

Did Willard even make it to the door?

Was he holding himself together?

Who told him to go away?

Who told him Indians weren't allowed?

Who told him this time?

This was the hospital where you had

pneumonia, where you were treated well am I

making any of this up?

Can I write this down on paper?

Do you remember how it felt

when he telephoned you with the news?

Dad?

Do you mind if I ask these questions?

Do you need a couple of minutes?

Should I call back another time?

III.

Driving into Fort Yates

His forehead beads sweat

along the brow bones, near the nose.

It is early evening, 1968,

the towel he holds to his stomach

turns crimson and crowds the old Chevy

with stench of blood.

Outside the car, pheasants fly up near

the wheels, flap and move off toward a purple butte.

The sun is giving up, sighing and turning

his shoulder away.

Willard begins to feel weak. He shakes, grips

the wheel and keeps driving.

Twenty-seven miles to the Indian hospital.
Twenty-seven miles from the hospital
on Standing Rock Reservation
where he was refused admittance.
The hospital in the town where he went to school
where he grew up learning the rules.

He closes his eyes to the serpent pain
when it curls around his neck.
He sees the first lights of Fort Yates
and judges how far away it is.
He can tell whether or not he will make it.
The car's engine coughs along.
There is no one on earth except him,
there is no road but this one.

PART II

SILK DRAGONS

We sit in the kitchen,

fluorescent hum of midnight between us,

and talk around years of nameless sex,

screen doors left open and banging.

Jokes like slipcovers over everything.

I want to know why, but do not ask.

He wants to tell me.

He does not.

Family blames the war.

He came back a little less married.

Found out the first time

he looked at her, knew it was all over,

knew it wasn't.

I never knew her.

And something about chemicals in that war.

Rashes. I don't know; I was a child.

I remember a Korean jacket

covered with silk dragons,

their wild tails curling.

Smell of horse hair and sweat.

The coffee boils to nothing.

"But you have your life," I say.

"Give it a rest, Kate.

This ol' cowboy's dust.

I'm walking to Kansas City."

And he does as we sit there,

all night talking, together,

in the cream and sugar kitchen

and welcome him home.

LOOKING FOR QUIXOTE

In this summer sculpture garden
a life-size nag leans,
a driftwood skeleton
looking for a listening ear.
Bronze driftwood, the artist's secret,
the curious illusion of art.
People file past, some never see
the horse's truth, some
pay no attention at all.

But in winter I stand,
snow in my collar,
and look through the ribs
to the bare hedge beyond.
Look at this horse again, at every horse

I've ever been afraid to love.

I stand, stinging in the hollow cold,

and see the ribs move,

and hear a heart.

This is no secret.

This horse is cold and tired

and stranded—

I hold golden corn in my pockets,

the warm barn in the palm of my hand.

CRYING AT THE MOVIES

Pictures on the shelf of a life,

half in—half out of the hermit's shell,

trying like hell to figure out

what it's hiding and when it's going to get on

with living. It isn't an easy black and

white sort of thing.

A plant in the corner gets

enough water, but it doesn't bloom anyway.

Christ girl, you are a romantic.

The celluloid apartment reveals no more than

necessary, the thin hand that wishes to stroke love

like everyone else,

wishes to sleep on the shoulder of security.

Buildings get bombed.

Things thrown out of windows in frustration.

Unrequited love, murders, the usual stuff.

Put your hand to your cheek. Feel the tears.

Know that you are more than simply alive

and able to walk out the door to the street.

A QUESTION OF BALANCE

I saw that pheasant week after week
as the sun crawled over my dashboard,
every morning the same rooster near the deep ditch.
Familiar with the highway's shoulder,
he followed his pebbled routine close to my wheels.

They used to be everywhere.
On long car rides over Dakota gravel roads,
I counted pheasants in tawny grass;
two hundred and twelve, two hundred and thirteen ...
the earth-painted birds thriving mile after mile.

I remember my father and his brothers
smiling against an autumn sun,
holding strings filled with limp birds like dead laundry.

They said hunting kept things balanced,

otherwise too many would starve.

I touched feathers and closed vacant eyes.

I'd expected this bird's death for weeks.

But commuting in at dawn, I passed his stiff corpse

on the gravel border and felt the gap

of an old-world warrior gone,

back where the song begins near Bear Butte,

back where prayers help lift the dead

to where they belong.

EMPTY HOUSE

Try the back door, no

the window with the mouth

full of witch's teeth,

crawl in cautiously,

and build a warm nest.

You will be safe there.

Curl around yourself, remember how

to pull back into the dream of amniotic memory.

Try the window below the crows

perched on the eaves waiting

for more than your arrival.

Waiting, because that's what crows do.

Slip past them. Move inside.

It is cold and getting colder.

TOLL BRIDGE

It seems the highway is always

under construction.

Workers roll hot pavement over pavement,

painting white lines,

filling pot holes.

I collect the fare,

play Captain-May-I

with the commuters.

"Yes, you may. And

come back soon.

Fifty cents, please.

An extra twenty-five for the trailer."

Don't tell me how Dad's trying

to get along again, or

that she's feeling better and maybe

there's something I can do.

Let me put in my hours

and be on my way.

Jesus, I'm not the bridge;

I just take the quarters.

PARENTS

There's all this dismembering going on
like a slaughterhouse on the southern prairie.
He'll cut off hers. She'll chew off his.
It isn't healthy, this need to physically separate.
This dealing out the cards of their fate.
You are an adult.
You tell them to go to their rooms.
Mommy, in the attic. Daddy, downstairs.
Tell them to string cobwebs from the rafters.
Do something useful, you say.
Gather dust, do anything.
They sulk off—they hate each other,
but they love you like a soft bed,
an old mattress to sink into and sleep.

Their lives are melting on the projector,
film curling from the hot white light.
They want to forget. They want to fight.
You want to burn down the house
in the quiet of the night.

BROTHER ON A SPUN GLASS WEB

He holds on, the delicate web

gives way, cuts fingers,

bleeds way back to second grade, to third.

Year after year of shadow love,

of promises and punishments,

of sadness and sickness,

and one more tries.

He sits in the chair

and tries to keep his body contained

in its shell, grabs like hell

at the web that surrounds him

in its tenuous strands.

He holds on, but it breaks and slices;

he begins to bleed again.

I am the oldest sister who moved out

when he was a baby.

I reach out for the first time.

I wrap my arms around the man

and try to move back in,

try to tell the heart to slow down,

try to talk it out of exploding.

I dance to slow the blood,

dance with heavy feet,

dance with an electric longing called love.

POLITICS

I never said it couldn't happen.
Spiders trick their lacy net
across the Mississippi, and
you and I picnic there
on pears and strong cheese—
forty feet above the water.
I am dressed like a rock star.
I am drinking too much.
I am telling very bad jokes.

You laugh anyway,
tell me you are married, and
employed, and a parent, tell me
you are up for election, will I

vote for you? Will I

put a sign on my lawn?

Will I ever slow down?

LUCY

If dreaming is remembering, Lucy,
how close do I come to the volcanic heat
of your world? You, the riddle
we thought we solved when your bones
were unearthed, preserving the answer
to the earliest human, the first mother
yet to be found.
Your pelvis, an open butterfly like mine,
knew childbirth, felt the cycles of the moon.
Your feet like my feet, but smaller,
your hands, my hands.
We have touched children, you and I.
The earth is still here, struggling to survive.
And when I dream of you in the deep night
my tongue speaks in guttural sounds,

asks you female questions, invites you

to sit by my fire. What is locked in the brain

of the past? What do I carry around with me still?

What do we all know?

What have we always known?

MADE IN CHINA

She paints one more mouth,
adds Santa's eyes, stretches
her back to alter the flowing
river of pain from too much sitting—
her daughter and grandchild still
at home, sick with the flu, perhaps
she comes down with it herself.
The crowded walk home
reminds her she has a name of her own,
a street to turn down, a front door.
She sighs, exhaling the gray night,
the United States of America,
and all the dead evergreen trees standing
an ocean away. Behind her eyelids

is a miniature image of the stout porcelain man;

she leaves it outside, with her boots,

and crosses the stoop to her life.

ISLAND

It takes two days

of backstroke

to get away from here,

spitting fish

from my mouth

when they accidentally

sigh and dart

the same time I do.

Salt crusts

on my brown brows,

my forehead grows red

and blisters.

The wild sun confuses me.

I see Medusa hair in the sky

as spirals of heat

lick the blue void.
Her center turns black
and spreads like oil
faster than I can swim.
My legs are not tired.
I left them on shore,
on the island, with you
and a cooking fire.
Stir the boiling stew
in the pot,
lick your fingers
and eat, eat your fill!
Don't wait for me—
I won't be back
in time.
(I won't be back.)

MAYBE I'M DANCING

in the North woods shouldering Canada,

the lakes full of possibility,

the flies electrifying the cabin with sound.

Maybe Billie Holiday and a trumpet

slide past my ear and I'm wearing silk

and red, red lipstick,

my hair long and crimped.

Maybe it is forty-five years ago.

It is the first time I've been alive.

My ears buzz with music;

I am boozy drunk, a full

four counts ahead of the shadows

and no place to go

that would be

quite like this.

I WANT, I HAVE

I want a porch where I can watch the birds,

a four-season porch, able to breathe in summer.

I want a dog with a trick.

The dog would sun in the porch all winter.

I have a black and white photo of myself

as a child with my brother. We are happy.

I have a color photo of you over my desk.

You are smiling and watering my words as they grow.

I want a letter from Africa. Someone I once knew

could have traveled there and thought of me.

I want to drink Retsina in Sitia.

In Sitia, with you and the sea's blue touch.

I have a silver dollar from when I was four,

four and afraid of riding ponies.

I have the first letter you wrote to me from your bathtub.

The letter I used to read every night.

I want jungle trees to grow in my living room,

to grow and remind me of spring.

I want to swim under the lake's ice.

Under the ice, where I can dive into black pressure.

I have a dream every night that all those I love die.

They die, and in the morning, I get them all back.

In the morning, I pull you close, and all the others

are back, and I want to stay awake forever.

SUBTEXT

She said that I blame my life

on whatever goes into my body,

as if my life

were in need of blame.

I stand in her kitchen,

hands around a cup of carrot soup,

look away for self-preservation.

Dusty yellow light edges the clouds.

The back door stands slightly ajar.

I think I may hear thunder,

but perhaps I listen too intently.

In spite of us, festive

conversation blossoms

in the next room.

SISTER

I want to say don't worry

everything will . . . I want to be kind.

But your street sits empty

like a frozen stream,

fish suspended between seasons,

life suspended between what is

and what should be.

His life is not driving by in a car.

You hold on to the white windowsill

and remember the river

as you go down for the fourth time;

I want to give you air.

I want to breathe into your lungs

everything that you may need.

I want to say don't . . . I want

to be kind.

I want to be the car you are looking for;

I want to ease your mind. Sisters are like that;

they will climb behind the wheel of anything

and offer to drive you home.

WE HAVE NEVER LIVED

This house wasn't built,
brick upon brick,
hand, labor, cement—
wasn't here, ever.
No rooms, no history.

This child, sleeping, head turned,
open mouth on flannel sheet,
was never born, never loved.
We have nothing to lose.

NOT THIS ONE

I could write a whole book
about the pain of it—about
the violence soldiered in
newsprint columns like tombstones,
like last words bubbling
from a victim's mouth.
Not tonight. I want to live
long enough to grow old,
to feel less at times than others
and to notice the salmon geranium
on my neighbor's front step,
the potted one that has been there
all summer.

ANNIVERSARY POEM

And just what do I say
about ten years of this waking up
shoulder to shoulder still
holding hands?
Good morning and I love you, yes,
but they are the easy ones.
If I tell you I would stay alive
in some prison camp
years with my bones clacking
under translucent skin—
years writing poems on flour sacks
and hiding them from the guards
with the hope of seeing you again—
believe me.
If I tell you I would rebuild this house,

brick upon brick, if a quake pulled it down,

with the hopes you would

sleep with me under its heavenly roof—believe me.

And if I say you are the one

who taught me to breathe,

the one who let go of the string

and said fly! and I did—

believe me.

PART III

THE END OF THE ROAD

The road just ended, that's how he tells it.
Driving along, pavement turned to gravel,
turned to dirt, and then nothing but prairie grass
and miles of blue-clouded sky.
It was 1961. The car was old; the fenders and hood
curved and sensuous as a Renoir nude.
She remembers. She was four and sat in the back seat
while her parents studied a worn map.
They couldn't turn back now. They were going somewhere
and wanted to get there. They sat and talked quietly,
thinking this was funny, this was a shame.
The girl was thinking about being a princess
with a court full of yellow canaries at her beck and call.
The birds sang to her as small mice braided her hair
and told her she was beautiful. She had her own kingdom.

Her brothers were not sitting next to her

complaining about the heat.

When the horses arrived over a small hill waving with grass,

her father saw them first. Wild horses.

Told everyone to be still. Slowly, like caterpillars

crawling the length of her arm, they approached the car.

"Curious," her father whispered.

The horses surround them,

peering in windows, snorting and stomping.

A white stallion, his mane electric in the breeze,

licked the windshield and someone flinched.

The horses bolted—ran over a wrinkle of ridge

as quickly as they had come.

"Salt," her father said. "They were looking for salt."

She closed her eyes and followed them, slinging

handfuls of white crystals from the pockets of her dress,

walking barefoot back to her castle.

SHE WAS ALONE

when the phone rang, when
the news curled out of the receiver
like smoke from a lazy pipe.
She held the plastic in her hand
long after the officer said it a second time.
The machine's impatient beeping
finally reminded her
that the phone was off the hook.

She was off the hook. No more
mothering a man who never knew her.
His dark hands would lie still
to forget the tortured past.
No more twisted nights
when she sat near his bed and sang

lullabies in a second language.

He had been a weight around her neck.

A boarder. Some income. It was easier

to cook meals for two. He came to this country

and fell off the edge of the world.

She picked him up. Taught him the word for flower,

for sunset. They took long walks when he was well

and almost always got lost.

Years ago in Vietnam, he told her,

he had a house and a woman and an ox.

He had gods and reasons to be alive.

Now the voice on the phone says he walked into traffic.

He died instantly. No one else was hurt.

She remembers that last part. She imagines

a herd of horses is running over her body.

They pound into her and keep on going.

SILVERTIP

This isn't about a horse or an auctioneer's babble,

isn't about a Shetland pony with a silver mane

and one glass eye, isn't about me,

a four-year-old girl riding on his back,

always afraid because he spooked easily;

you needed to talk when walking up to him,

and always on his good side, and I was afraid to ride.

Isn't about that day we sold him,

and the auctioneer rambled words

to the night corners of the sale barn,

not about summer heat,

or the almost sweet smell of sweat. All the farmers

smiling at the little girl with long hair. Why was I there?

Perhaps this is about confusion.

See the little girl riding a horse,

see how gentle the pony is,

see the little girl holding the horn,

think of your little girl or little boy,

buy this horse.

It isn't about my father telling me to climb off,

and then, in the noise and confusion, I stood there,

transfixed by the crowd and he was gone.

I found myself surrounded by dirty white lambs

to my waist; this isn't about them.

Maybe it's about being pushed from all sides

by a family that still can't stop going in circles. I am the one

in the middle. The others holler and bargain for a fair price.

One man in overalls offered me a hand

over the chain link fence, yelled that I could climb

that high, and I did. All those farmers smiling.

Later Dad gave me a silver dollar for my bravery.

I still have that coin. I am not brave anymore.

I listen, and listen, and circle around, letting everyone

get what they came for.

YOU KNOW

"...old alchemical riddles are
solved in the dreams of men
who marry other women and
think of us."
—Diane Wakoski

I could dance circles

around this conversation—

why is it you say

my strength

makes you want to sleep with me,

then you go away

to have nightmares

of being overpowered?

The escape of men

baffles me.

And let's talk about

all the clear answers

intelligent women hold

in the seashells of their brains—

men lean close

trying to hear the call of the sea

in our ears, but

they never get close enough—

such wisdom is sacrificed

for a high tide

and another life

with a woman

who does not contain such power.

But the women with the music

keep dancing,

dancing and waving their arms

in circles like silk kite tails—

they know about the waves,

and the tides, and

have been living with it

all their lives.

The hell of the thing is,

they know they aren't missing much—

men who run like shadows to escape

everything they desire

just don't seem worth mourning.

But intelligent women dream too,

late at night,

alone with their oceans,

and sometimes mythical gods tell them

things they already know,

tell them that something is missing.

EQUESTRIAN

The black mare wears snow,
a saddle blanket across
the desire of her back.
She stands still,
ass to the wind.

The snow keeps falling.
The man in the wool coat
and warm boots delivered hay
hours ago, drove off
in a pickup and turned left
at the county road
when he could have
come here.

I would have lied to him anyway,

repeating shadows from dreams, giving

every assurance it didn't matter, singing

every line that gave him room

to walk away;

I would have climbed on,

wanting passion to be enough,

and ridden that cold horse home.

CONFESSION

It isn't like I leave my shades open at night.
I worry the most about noises that come back
again and again. Why would I write about that
when haunting echoes make a woman
as vulnerable as an infant, as the child
of the man who opened the car window and
tossed the kid out so he'd shut up?

You have to keep yourself out of it—leave
the razor sharp nights when walls were screaming
and your parents were on the other side
hacking away at every positive thing—*you can't
say that.* Make up something about the way
the river seduces the shore. How one lone bird
ruffles its feathers and settles down on a nest

like a bag lady on the courthouse steps.

The boy is paralyzed for life. Already wears a halo
to mend bones, but bones can't help him now.
He says little, remembers the feeling of flight
before he hit the ground, remembers
the echo of horror, once again, that noise,
the cry of the car as it screeched away and left him,
young , face down in the grass.

Confession. I don't know the boy in the newscast.
I sit on the hood of the car going 60 miles an hour
and take notes, trying to tell you some damn thing
about being a child.

RIDING HORSES

I was afraid to ride.

It was a religion with him.

The blanket first, then

each leather piece in place,

three fingers under the saddle's front cinch.

Every time he talked me through it,

I saw the horse's hide twitch with flies,

my stomach in its own spasms.

He helped me mount. I felt muscle

and power wide between my thighs.

I knew she could buck me, knew

she wanted to. It was hot August

and those flies. He wouldn't let me get down.

Again and again, "You won't fall off. See.

Hold the horn. She isn't going to hurt you."

I was afraid of horses. He loved them.

On the freeway now, in thick summer heat,

I think of those years. My white knuckles grab the rush hour,

twisting the old memory like hot iron.

We all need someone to blame.

YOU KNOW WHERE I LIVE

What is so difficult?
The phone see the phone
pick it up my number
is as easy as any other you
know it by heart it is written
on the inside of your wrist.

Instead you curse me
stand in your bathroom
look in a mirror
that threatens to drown you.
You cannot swim you refuse
a life vest you want to
struggle and yell till the shore
is lined with helping hands.

And if I call then what?

My hands are limp fish I cannot

hold anything these days I

will not walk on my hands

for you no circus show no

rescue squad racing to your door

you know where I live.

THE PSYCHIC

Today you called, said you'd asked her about my career,
my photo there on the table before you,
between your hands and hers.

Two months ago, at a poetry reading, I tried,
once again, to impress you. We talked about the psychic,
about her version of your life.

Later, on the backbone of Chicago's downtown,
racing for Midway to catch your flight home,
we drove through tense rain.

After you flew out,
on the hood of my wet car,
I sat with a headache

and cried for no good reason.

She told you good news today, like honey on the tongue,
golden harp strings between the bee and me,
and I would, and someone, somewhere would.

How do I feel about that? you ask across the map
Of telephone poles. *Like I've always wanted.*
Like I've always feared.

What about the house you are building?
May I write my words on your walls?
May I write whatever I want?

And if this prediction never happens,
then what can I put down on paper?
What will you be happy to read?

I am perched in the branches of a protected pine.
I am writing again.
In that photo, was I smiling?

ABOUT THE GODS

Go out to the yard,

light the coals for a barbecue, buy wine.

Play chess by the edge edge edge of the lake

and talk about last night against velvet—

checkmate.

Play out your strategy, play it out

but do not tie my hands into your game.

The greenest grass grows nearest the water.

I sit in the lovely softness

and what is that?

And who touches the lids of my eyes at dawn

to share the foggy morning jewel?

Who fills my lungs with calm calm joy

at such a young world?

Who teaches the spider to weave
her lacy home in the rafters
where she rests on the edge
of the answer?

Who pipes warm air into my newborn's stiff lungs,
until the chest expands, unfolds
and blossoms, the tulip bowl of the lungs!

At night I do not pray to the gray ceiling
and count my finger's bones—I do not
and I do, and in the morning
the sun rises, much more
than a burning globe of scientific heat.

*

---

*   After D. H. Lawrence

SITTING BULL'S BONES

They are back there, in my childhood,

not by the trailer tangled in tumbleweeds,

not by the side of the road, not in

the dirt yard where I played house.

Not in this photograph of me

in a white hooded sweatshirt, holding my dusty dolls.

Some say the Sioux leader's bones

are hidden in the country,

buried beneath an ancient rock

between McLaughlin and Bull Head,

those reservation towns with the names of military men

who dreamed about being heroes. Dreamed

the Indians' old ways would disappear.

Used guns when they weren't asleep

to do their dreaming for them.

Sitting Bull was awakened from his bed at dawn,

pulled outside and shot; his crime was giving hope

to a people with little hope left.

This crime is still punished today.

Lock your windows at night.

Sleep with your back to the wall.

Pay attention to the patterns of clouds.

I AM NOT BRAVE

And suddenly at fifty-three
I realize it, take a bow
to no one, empty theater,
show over, end of game,
do not collect.

I have not been honest, or
maybe I have been, but
things change,
and my truth now has
a little decaf mixed in,
a couple of swear words, a
sigh, and my truth is
no longer true.

What did I want anyway?
An award? Some
pat on the back
for years without sleep, years
without years, a hug?
I am not brave. I
may never have been
brave. I am not,
truth be told, the person
I never was.

REASONS

The wool for my loom

must come from way back,

when I still knew how to saddle a horse

and life existed from one ride to the next.

I started riding horses when I was six

and not skipping rope.

By nine, my hands galloped through long hair

gathering their own words.

When I was fourteen, my family sold the horses

and moved to another state.

I got my period, read the women poets

and worried about going insane.

The horses were gone,

the festival of childhood,

the old hope for first blood in my panties.

I write horses because of two brown eyes

as big as riverbank plums,

the eyes of the pony that looked only for me

at every sound of the barn door.

I weave horses in and out of my life

because there is nothing like holding tight to a mane

when you feel yourself falling.

RIDE SOUTH

When I have ridden all day,

and my legs move with the lungs of the mare,

when her legs become my legs

for all intents and purposes,

I can ride south and not look back—

not at the gravel behind me,

not at the grassy house disappearing,

not at the book

in which I have written down

my life.

PUBLICATION CREDITS

"Indelible Drums" *Streamlines*, 7-2 (1987).

"Silk Dragons," "Riding Horses," and "She Was Alone" in Loft-McKnight Awards anthology, *Night Talk* (Fall, 1991).

"Long Walk on Standing Rock" *Nimrod* Vol 35-1 (Fall/Winter 1991).

"Toll Bridge" *Sing Heavenly Muse!* (1993, Vol. 20).

"Sitting Bull's Bones" in the *Black Bear Review*, Winners of the Sixth Annual International Poems of Social Concern Poetry Competition (1994, Vol. 18).

"Lucy" in *I Am Becoming the Woman I've Wanted*, an anthology from Papier-mâché Press, winner of an American Book Award (1994).

"Silk Dragons" in *The Hermit Kingdom*, an anthology about the Korean War from The Center for the Study of the Korean Conflict and Kendall-Hunt Publishing (1995).

"About the Gods" in *Prayers to Protest: Poems That Center and Bless Us*, an anthology from Pudding House Publications (1995).

"Permission" in *Writing Our Way Out of the Dark*, an anthology from Queen of Swords Press (1995).

"Confession" in Rag Mag (1996).

"She Was Alone" in *A Contemporary American Survey: The Unitarian-Universalist Poets*, from Pudding House Publications (1996).

ABOUT THE AUTHOR

Kathleen Patrick is a poet and fiction writer with an MA in Creative and Professional Writing whose work includes poetry, short stories, and novels. She writes for adults, teens, and children. Her work has received honors from the Academy of American Poets as well as Loft-McKnight Awards in poetry and fiction.

Airmail: A Story of War in Poems was her first published book. *Mercy* is her first coming-of-age novel, and *Anxiety in the Wilderness* is her first book of short stories. *Perfume River*, is a contemporary novel about searching for happiness in trying times. Her latest novel, *The Shoe Box Waltz* is a gripping multidimensional novel that will leave you unsettled until the very end. *So Many Wings,* her last collection of poetry, was published earlier this year. *Wild Horses* is her latest book of poetry.

Patrick describes herself as an "anxious optimist" full of hope; her books reflect that optimism and the importance of love and family. She taught middle school for over twenty years and said teaching seventh grade was the best job ever. She lives in Minnesota and enjoys writing, reading, traveling, and watching college basketball. She was once the hula hoop champion of Osceola County.

facebook.com/kathleenpatrick

instagram.com/@patrickpoetry

amazon.com/author/kathleenpatrick

PLEASE REVIEW THIS BOOK

Reviews help authors more than you might think. Sometimes they even help readers decide what to read. If you liked *Wild Horses,* please consider writing a review wherever you purchased this book and including it on your social media platforms. It can be a few words or a few short sentences. I would greatly appreciate it.

WORDS AND REVIEWS

Airmail: A Story of War in Poems

"I read it in one sitting and thoroughly enjoyed (if that's the right word) every poem." —Tim O'Brien, author of *The Things They Carried*

"*Airmail: A Story of War in Poems*...is a great example of how letters and conversations can be turned into stunning poetry. Patrick shares the words and thoughts of seven uncles who served in the military, five of them in Southeast Asia during the American war in Vietnam. ...It's always cool to see letters sent home from war turned into poems. They become letters from America sent back to America. Kathleen Patrick shows us what it can look like when it's done poetically and done right." —Bill McCloud, The VVA Veteran magazine

"Love the voice and reading pace. It's great, and the content is amazing. I am a Vietnam vet and I can relate 100%. Thanks for taking the time to do this project." —J.I.

"Some very strong work here, grounded in correspondence that Kathleen had with her uncles while they served in Vietnam, and also in their correspondence with their parents, subsequent interviews, etc. An amazing piece of work. This is the best war lit I have read since *The Things they Carried* by Tim O'Brien." —Peter Ludlow, author of *Living Words*, Oxford University Press

"A story that stays with you. I read a lot of historical fiction surrounding WWI and II, but this collection of poems highlighting the perspectives of a family living through Vietnam was just as beautiful. Reading poetry framed as letters by young men wanting to serve and the loved ones they left behind was powerfully written and even more powerful in the things that were left unsaid. This is a collection that should be read slowly, absorbing the words from each letter. —A. C.

"Wow…Honestly, I don't read a lot of poetry and didn't think I would like it. However, I loved it; it sucked me right in, and I thought it was beautifully done." —L.M.

"This collection distills so much family history into consumable little poems that will leave you wrecked in the best possible way. A beautiful read." —H.C.

Mercy

"*Mercy* is a phenomenal young adult coming of age story that will capture the hearts of readers of all ages!"—K.C.

"*Mercy* is a story of adolescence, but adults would love it as well. It explores the emotional turbulence inherent in dysfunctional families and what it takes to move from dysfunction to love to mercy. Any book that can make me cry and laugh out loud is a winner. *Mercy* is a winner!"—J.C.

"A coming of age, found family, young adult novel. A heartwarming story about a twelve-year-old girl named Sadie who finds the family she always craved in her uncle on a farm. After Sadie's mother struggles with gambling addiction after her father's departure, Sadie has a life of instability and worry. Great short read. The only thing I have to say bad about the story is that it simply isn't long enough!" —K.F.

"Mercy was just a great story and a breath of fresh air!" —L.P.

Anxiety in the Wilderness

"A book of short stories that can only be described as bittersweet. Some parts defiantly pulled at my heartstrings. The author herself said the book was written over a long time period. This comes across in the different scenarios in which the characters are involved in. Each a little exceptional tale of it's own. I especially liked the crossover of characters. I am now patiently waiting for a full novel set in the Iowa wilderness!" —K. F., Goodreads review

"The poetic language of the stories lends a warmth to the storytelling that helps to bring the characters to life. Each story describes a different human worry or anxiety that we all may have experienced at some point in our lives; therefore, each story is relatable in its own way….Short stories are a disappearing art form, and Patrick demonstrates why we should keep them around. There is no grandiosity of language that detracts from the storyline or from the artful character descriptions. Characters navigate their way through their predicaments one day at a time. The poignant vignettes showcase the rawness of various human emotions, much like a snapshot of an expert photographer."—B. M., Goodreads Review

"I loved this book! From beginning to end the characters smack of realism and you can see people you know or yourself in them. I wish it were the first book in a series of ten—because I wanted more!"

Perfume River

"It is a beautifully written novel with deep feelings. It is the kind of book that wins prize…" -Evelyn Singer

"Patrick's prose is smooth, even, and consistent. As with her other work, her use of words is sparse and succinct leaving the reader to indulge in their own imaginings of the space and events. The pauses and silences are evocative." -J.S.

"Absolutely loved the main character! Great read!" -K. K.

"I enjoy Kathleen Patrick's concise descriptive abilities sprinkled with emotional and intellectual truths." -C. T.

"The characters are well drawn, and the story is both touching and humorous. Worth the read!" -E. S.

The Shoe Box Waltz

"*The Shoe Box Waltz* is the story of lives intertwined, each one shaped by the others it touches. Each of these lives is in turn shaped by single defining moments, a moment that we never expect to possess such impact. This is a novel of the power of such encounters, seemingly so fleeting and unimportant at the time, as they become amplified… Patrick's prose is literary; thoughtful and evocative, stealthily drawing emotion from the reader." —J. L.

"The Shoe Box Waltz by Kathleen Patrick is an enthralling novel that at times wraps its arms around to comfort the reader and at other times hits the reader with raw emotions. This book continues to showcase Patrick's ability to observe the human condition and represent it in poetic language that leaves the reader knowing exactly what the characters are going through along their lifelong journeys…Patrick does what she does best: she creates an environment of empathy for her characters that brings the readers a little closer to the truth of the human condition." –Brandee Miller , Goodreads review

The Shoebox Waltz by Kathleen Patrick is a captivating novel that follows the life of Cora Daneli, a young woman in search of adventure. Set against the stunning backdrop of the Italian coast, this book takes readers on a thrilling journey that explores the depths of human emotions and the unforeseen paths life can lead us down. –Travel Through Books, Goodreads review

"The characters are fascinating and I love the sense of voice through the narrative and dialogue. The traumatic scenes are handled with power and grace; it's a difficult subject but Patrick moves deftly through those scenes.

The code-switching in tenses and voices was disconcerting at first but I caught up. Patrick has raised the raised the bar on the "unreliable narrators" concept. A bit of an emotional roller coaster and well worth the read!" –Sarah P. Blanchard, Author of *Drawn from Life* and *river, horse, morning*

So Many Wings

"Kathleen Patrick's poetry is very good. 'Letter to a Granddaughter' is incredible… I like her metaphors… I seldom read work I like so much." –Kathleen Iddings

[*So Many Wings*] "reveals slices of life, all the joy, fear, love and sadness that makes up the human condition. Patrick continues to do what she does best: she showcases what it means to be human. Each poem reveals its own story; however, once you read through the collection, another story emerges. You can admire the fine detail of each poem and then step back and appreciate the tapestry as a whole.

We all consist of many parts: granddaughter, mom, wife, friend, etc. And each one of these parts are a chapter in our journey through life.. The chapters are not always comfortable parts of our lives, but they add to what makes each of us unique. Yet, Patrick brings such empathy into her poems, that almost anyone can relate." –Brandee Miller, Goodreads review

"How does a woman grow? What does she make of the complicated moments of her life, some lovely, some dark? In *So Many Wings*, her second collection, poet Kathleen Patrick collects those moments and lets them cook until the lush evocations of the sky and fields of her Dakota home transform them into poetry." –Elizabeth Bourque Johnson

"Lovely, lyrical poems span the breadth of experience. What a lovely collection of poems! Patrick pulls it all together: the fears and joys of childhood and too-early adulthood; a grief that comes through loss, but also through experience; the complexities of love and desire…Read these poems. They will speak to you." –Sarah Blanchard, Author of *Drawn From Life* and *river, horse, morning*

FREE SHORT STORY!

Sign up for my mailing list at the address below and get a free short story! "Anxiety in the Wilderness" is the title story from my collection of short stories by the same title.

https://patrickpoetry.com/

A sample from

So Many Wings

I.

"And something started in my soul,
fever or forgotten wings,
and I made my own way."

"Poetry" by Pablo Neruda, 1964

The Problem with Poetry

If it itches you can't scratch it,

only write about scratching,

and in writing it,

make the scratchy feeling

only itch more.

And if it is too troublesome,

the poem is said to work,

like engines work in cars, and filaments connect

the necessary things in light bulbs.

And if it works, folks seem to like it

and sit scratching and squirming

while they read the measured lines.

Another problem is weight.

Poems want to be perfect,

like fashion models or carats of gold,

not too heavy (no one would bother)

but heavy enough, so they don't blow over.

Poems want to be just right,

long enough to make you itch for more,

but no unnecessary words,

only the electric ones

that bridge the gap between words

and whatever it is

that makes a poem a poem.

A poem changes us; it

gives us a push, lets us jump in,

barefoot and giddy.

Poetry causes trouble.

Poetry can be a pain in the ass.

The problem with poetry

is you want to scratch an itch,

so you write. Then you read it,

and something stares back at you

from the paper. It is a photograph of you,

a candid shot before you wake up,

eyes closed like shades against empty glass.

Your hair is a mess. Your mouth is open.

You have never looked so tired in your life.

In Iris

(Fleur-de-Lys c.1899 by Robert Reid)
I find her there
in the broken-color
garden of paint.
This pastel-skinned woman,
concealed by a crowd of iris.

What brings her to the garden?
She may be hiding
amongst the tall heads of blossom,
everything dabbed lavender and white.
Or perhaps she sits here afternoons
and tries to remember.

>   A frayed collar (or was it?)
>   Two birds on the sill.
>   Spiced Burgundy after walking.

Some might say she is growing
into a flower herself.
I like this version best.
Her fingers on the verge
of budding green,
her eyes blossoming
as instinct turns her
toward the sun.

Never mind the man in the coat,

the days of cold winter.

There is more now, I want to say.

Forget how the sill held new snow.

And the pair of birds,

forget the birds.

1942

My father's father died by lightning,

and the tractor kept circling

the empty field.

His mother, in curlers and an apron,

took the old car searching for him

as drops of rain darkened the dust.

The sky turned black,

South Dakota black and angry,

and he remembers it all.

Seven then, one of seven,

old enough to remember,

to be confused about crying.

And after he heard the news,

after the storm had passed,

in the haymow alone, sun through the boards,

he listened to pigeons

on the rafters, so many wings,

so far away above his head.

Away From This Place

Dusty ankles and feet swing

between porch and grass, green with summer.

Near the creek full of bullheads,

a sack swing hangs

with straw and thick rope

that can fly over the water

like a glider on a down draft,

and then the lip, catching it,

pulling up and more of the same,

back over the water tail, curling through

the pasture, back over

the brown water headed for the Missouri,

headed away from this place.

The screen door is torn, mother's voice inside

cusses at the flies.

It is hot enough for swimming,

for losing your own face under water to the bubbles.

"Can't we? This once?"

But the fields need turning, need hands

and seed, father's reply.

Every lake is worlds away,

and we haven't been in the creek

since we can't remember when.

In the shady apple grove,

we chain dandelion stems together,

linking one ankle to the other.

We are prisoners planning our escape.

Hiding

We knew the latch would keep,

knew the smell of dirt floors and oil,

old tires stacked high

in that nothingness.

Grandpa worked there fixing tractors,

mending pumps, changing tires

on the moss-green Ford.

You, one year older,

my uncle from that big family,

more a cousin, more a brother

with red hair. I wanted to kiss you;

I don't know why. I was seven or eight

and afraid of the dark.

You wanted to put a dead rat in my face,

swung it by the tail, screaming

"It's alive, it's alive, it's after you!

We were playing capture.

We were hiding from the rest of the world.

Later, at night, in your house,

I held my pee, afraid

of the slight sound of mice

scurrying across linoleum.

I pulled the covers over my face

and tried to think of other things.
Grandpa's praying voice reached me
from his room. He said the rosary
and began again.
I said nothing to anyone.

Coffee In the Evening

tastes twice,

a bitter cold

after company leaves.

Try the lock on the door,

return the phone

to its cradle,

smooth corners on rag rugs.

Outside a country owl

claims territory with long spectral cries.

The last car on gravel

parts the dark, leaving thick dust.

Follow the hallway

past shelves of books

to the novel that doesn't end

by the bed.

Cold coffee

in the evening quiet.

Above town,

July fireworks fill

an otherwise empty sky.

Boundary Waters

Islands, like big families

on the fourth, crowd the waters here,

green arms to their shorelines.

Hands quiver, (my hands, the trees,)

and fall into echo, fall back

as faint mist blankets me.

I am no one's mother!

Spray covers my lids and lashes.

I scream out of canoe bays

into the waved wind,

(or I do not scream

and the birds stay in the trees).

Waking

To wake with coffee,

a woman

with words to eat

and windows to open,

all I need.

Birds on the lake

call out in the sunshine.

There are animals here

that know where they are going.

In the spring,

there is dust

the rain must wash away,

and a newborn poem

wrinkled and wobbling

on young legs.

In early morning,

I collect words

for its first feeding.

A Sample from

Airmail: A Story of War in Poems

Note from the Author

When I was in the fourth grade, we had a map of Vietnam on
our kitchen wall. When my mother received an airmail letter,
she would walk to the map and move one of the stickpins to a
new location to see if one of her brothers was in harm's way
in some new hot spot or battle. I spent a lot of time worrying
about that map. I had five uncles in Southeast Asia during the
Vietnam War. Looking back, I guess it is a bit unusual for a
girl of nine or ten to write letters to her uncles in Vietnam, in
Thailand, in Cambodia. Even then, I knew that words could
make one feel better. I wrote about ice-skating at the park on a
cold Iowa Saturday. I wrote about school, basketball games,
and the books I was reading. My letters were written in wide,
awkward printing on little girl stationary. My uncles wrote
back and thanked me for writing.

Several years ago, one of those uncles wrote a line at the
bottom of his Christmas card. It said, "Someday I want to sit
down and tell you what it was like to be a young man going
off to war." I taped that card over my desk and began to
imagine their voices. Over the next years, I read hundreds of
letters that my mother and my grandfather had saved from the
boys, spanning many years. With the help of a Jerome Foun-
dation Grant and a Loft McKnight grant, I visited several of
the men in Mississippi, Alaska, and South Dakota and inter-
viewed them about their experiences. I recalled stories from
my childhood. They filled in the details. Some preferred not to
talk about it; others felt like it had released a great burden.

This manuscript is the result of those letters and those stories.
It is a book about going off to war, a book about coming back

home, and a book about those who are left behind. I took a few liberties with the facts simply because I do not know all there is to know, but I tried to retain the voices I have heard my whole life, the voices that ring true on parchment paper sent in airmail letters from all over the world.

I dedicate this book to those voices, to my family, and to every voice calling out at times of war: "I miss you. I love you. I wish I was home."

This book is dedicated to
Erma Young Smith, Joseph Edward Smith,
and their children.

Colleen Mae Smith Patrick

b. September 20, 1936

William Henry Smith
b. October 12, 1937

 United States Navy

 United States Air Force

Charles Leroy Smith
b. January 21, 1939

 United States Marines
d. August 22, 1992

 United States Army

Clement James Smith
b. June 15, 1942

 United States Navy
d. May 15, 2021

Robert Michael Smith
b. January 27, 1944

 United States Navy

Edward Joseph Smith
b. July 17, 1945

 United States Navy
d. March 5, 2014

Judith Fae Smith

b. November 30, 1946

Terrance David Smith
b. September 22, 1951

    United States Air Force

Delores Rae Smith Anderson

b. November 29, 1953

Timothy Allen Smith

b. March 21, 1956

    United States Army

Letter to Seven Uncles

Do you remember the smell of Lava soap
in the front porch when Dee and I sang "The Cruel War"?
Eddie's stern face in the mirror
when we sang his name instead of Johnny,
sang for your tears and the ceremony of good-bye?
Do you remember the coffee cans full of candy bars,
cookies and Dentine gum? Those CARE packages
from your mother's yellow kitchen
in the quiet days before the harvest?

I remember the map of Vietnam
on our kitchen wall in Iowa.
Each morning Mom listened to the news,
read blue airmail letters
and moved stick pins from one place
to another. I was nine and wanted
to stop that color-by-number war.

Grandma wrote to each of you every week.
She stood outside on the steps
when you came home on leave. Every time

you drove into that yard. Always outside waiting.

There is no one at the door now,

no one standing on the stoop

when the cars drive in or out.

And what of that?

What of the long nights when you tried to make sense

of a blank sheet of paper? Tried to think

of something safe to say?

Maybe I am standing at the door now.

I don't know what to say, but

I think it is important to write it down.

What do you remember?

What are you willing to tell?

I.
LEAVING

Photo Interpreter

I made sense of it

from the skies of Vietnam; looking down.

Above the menacing canopy

there was still all that sky

and God seemed, I don't know, closer.

It was my job to ferret out

the next disaster before it blew.

Photo mapping, target analysis,

bomb damage assessment.

I reported to Westmoreland each morning,

read those photographs, hell,

like a Gypsy reads an old man's palm.

Guess I was an expert at reading war from the sky.

But I tell you, I remember this one B-52 strike.

I was doing BDA, working my way through a bomb train;

I could see people standing around a crater,

could see the pattern of a building—the bomb

made a direct hit on a house. I saw

villagers standing around this gaping hole—

little kids stood next to parents

and hugged their unsteady legs.

I mean those kids looked like photos in my wallet.

That night, black and white glossies

floated over my bed;

ghosts that wouldn't go away.

I saw the high school newspaper,

the square Brownie camera that Sis used

to shoot the basketball team.

"We're weak at the corner of the court,"

I told her over breakfast eggs and homemade bread.

"I see a truck park half-a-mile from the border

but can't make out the intruding machinery."

"Follow the river," Sis said

with the gauzy voice of a dream.

"Let the shadows enhance the image."

Chain Link

Brother Bill was getting off a plane—

just in from Nam and I was going out.

Kadena Air Force Base. Okinawa.

Kind of strange that we met there like that

on the tarmac, he in the Air Force and me the Navy—

two brothers in with hundreds, hell thousands,

of soldiers coming and going.

I was looking around, waiting in line,

you do that a lot in the service,

watching them unload aluminum coffins

off this big C141 cargo plane

and then I saw Bill.

I wasn't that worried about being shipped out.

I'd been in a long time already;

I thought I was invincible—you know?

But then, I saw Bill and I knew for the first time—

just one look at his face—what I was in for

over there. They kept pulling those coffins

off the plane on pallets stacked five high.

I mean there's a hundred dead kids—

right there in one neat little pile;

they just shoved them out the back of that plane.

Two minutes, a hundred more and bam!

the plane's empty and taxis away in a hurry.

Bill runs over to me,

sticks his fingers through the chain link,

his line of men going one way and mine going the other.
"Jesus

Christ Bobby, it's good to see you."

And then there's this long pause and his eyes

go right through me.

"Just keep your head down little brother

and you'll be all right, you hear me?

Keep your head god damn on the ground."

Kind of funny, when you think about it.

Two farm boys a long way from home

standing at what could be the gates of hell—

touching each other's fingers

to be sure we're both alive.

ALSO BY KATHLEEN PATRICK

Airmail: A Story of War in Poems

Mercy

Anxiety in the Wilderness

Perfume River

The Shoe Box Waltz

So Many Wings